The Way of the Stars

Greek legends of the constellations

by Ghislaine Vautier
adapted by Kenneth McLeish

illustrated by Jacqueline Bezençon

CAMBRIDGE UNIVERSITY PRESS

Cambridge
London   New York   New Rochelle
Melbourne   Sydney

THE WAY OF THE STARS

For ten thousand years, the universe was torn by savage battles. On one side were the gods, led by Zeus and his brothers Hades and Poseidon. On the other were the Titans and their monster-allies the Giants. Their king was Kronos, and their war-leader was Atlas, lord of the kingdom of Atlantis.

At last Zeus and his brothers managed to beat Kronos and take his throne. Each brother had a single, powerful weapon, and they used them to help each other and win the war. Hades had a helmet of darkness, which made its wearer invisible. He put it on, crept into Kronos' palace and stole his weapons. Poseidon lifted his three-pronged trident-spear, and threatened to kill Kronos unless he surrendered. Zeus had the most terrible weapon of all: thunderbolts. He used them to keep the Titans and Giants at bay, and terrified them into ending the war.

Once the battle was over, each brother took a kingdom for his own. Poseidon ruled the sea; Hades' palace was deep in the Underworld, home of the dead; Zeus was ruler of the sky, and king of every god and mortal in the universe.

One by one, all the Titans and Giants who had fought the gods were punished. Soon only Atlas was left. For him, Zeus chose the heaviest punishment of all. He banished him to the edge of the world – the barren, desert place where all land ends. There Atlas had to stand for all eternity, balancing on his shoulders the arching, crushing weight of the sky above.

Although he punished Atlas, Zeus also rewarded him for his skill and bravery in the battle. He gave him a power granted only to one other god in the universe: Athene, goddess of wisdom. Atlas was told all the secrets of the constellations, and he helped mortals to understand the way of the stars, and their place and meaning in the heavens, for evermore.

Athene

CHARACTERS IN THE STORIES

Ariadne (ar-i-AD-ni). Princess of Crete. She fell in love with Theseus, and helped him escape after he killed the Minotaur.

Athene (ath-EE-ni). Goddess of wisdom.

Atlas (AT-lass). He helped the Titans fight the gods, and Zeus punished him by making him support the sky on his shoulders forever.

Cheiron (KAY-ron). King of the Centaurs, creatures half man half horse.

Demeter (dee-MEE-ter). Goddess of the earth and of all growing plants.

Dionysos (di-ON-i-soss *or* die-on-IE-soss). God of grapes and wine.

Gaia (GUY-a). Mother Earth, and mother of the Giants.

Hades (HAY-dees). Zeus' brother, king of the Underworld.

Hera (HEE-ra). Zeus' queen, goddess of marriage.

Herakles (HE-ra-klees). Son of Zeus and a mortal woman; one of the bravest of all Greek heroes.

Hermes (HER-mees). The messenger-god.

Hesperides (hess-PER-i-dees). Three nymphs who looked after the tree where the golden apples grew.

Jason (JAY-son). The hero who went to fetch the Golden Fleece. As a boy, he was brought up by Cheiron.

Ladon (LAY-don). Dragon-guardian of the garden of the Hesperides where the golden apples grew.

Medusa (me-DOO-sa). One of the three Gorgons. A single glance from her eyes would turn a mortal to stone.

Olympos (o-LIM-poss). The cloud-kingdom of the gods.

Pegasos (PEG-a-soss). Perseus' winged horse.

Perseus (PER-syooss). The hero who killed Medusa and rescued Andromeda.

Philomelos (fill-o-ME-loss). The mortal who invented the yoke.

Ploutos (PLOO-toss). Blind god of wealth.

Poseidon (pos-AY-don). Zeus' brother, god of the sea.

Theseus (THEE-syooss). The hero who killed the Minotaur.

Minotaur (MIN-o-tohr). A flesh-eating monster, half bull half man, which lived deep in the labyrinth in Crete.

Zeus (z-YOO-ss). King of gods and mortals. He often disguised himself and went to enjoy adventures among mortals down on earth.

GOLDEN APPLES

When Zeus married Hera and made her his queen, every god and spirit in the universe gave them wedding-presents. There were silken robes glittering with silver embroidery, jewelled armour, and chariots drawn by horses so fast that they outran the winds.

Gaia, Mother Earth, gave Hera the finest present of all. It was a golden apple tree. It grew in a garden high on a mountainside, and three mountain-spirits, the Hesperides, looked after it. They protected it from winter frost and gathered the heavy golden fruit at harvest-time.

Everyone in the universe, gods, mortals, giants and the nameless spirits of the darkness beyond the stars, was jealous of Hera's apple tree. She knew that unless she found it a protector, the tree or its dazzling fruit would be stolen. She chose Ladon, an unsleeping dragon, and made him guardian of the tree. He coiled his scaly body round the trunk; his eyes glowed red; his jaws gaped to show his flickering tongue and razor fangs. No one dared challenge him or go near the tree. Only the gentle Hesperides could stroke him, soothe him, and so pass by to tend the golden tree.

So the apple tree grew, safe in its garden, for a thousand years. It faded from memory, until it was no more than a beautiful legend in the minds of gods and mortals. Only Hera still cared for it. Every summer she visited the garden, picknicked on the grass with the Hesperides, and admired the growing, glittering fruit on the golden tree.

One other person remembered: a mortal, King Eurystheus of Mycenae in Greece. He sent the famous hero Herakles to kill Ladon and steal three golden apples. He hated Herakles, and hoped that Ladon would eat him before he ever reached the tree.

The dragon

Herakles climbed the steep mountain-side, and peered cautiously in across the garden wall. Ladon never slept; but he was basking in the hot sun, dozing. His head rested on his coils; his eyes were cloudy; his tail twitched lazily in the dust.

Herakles snatched his chance. He drew his sword, vaulted over the wall, and with one blow sliced off Ladon's head. He picked three apples and jumped back over the wall to safety.

What could Hera do? Herakles was Zeus' son, and she could do nothing to punish him. She turned the three Hesperides into trees: an elm, a poplar and a willow. Then, to punish Ladon for letting himself be tricked, she changed him into a constellation of stars, the Dragon, coiling and snaking forever across the sky.

THE CONSTELLATIONS

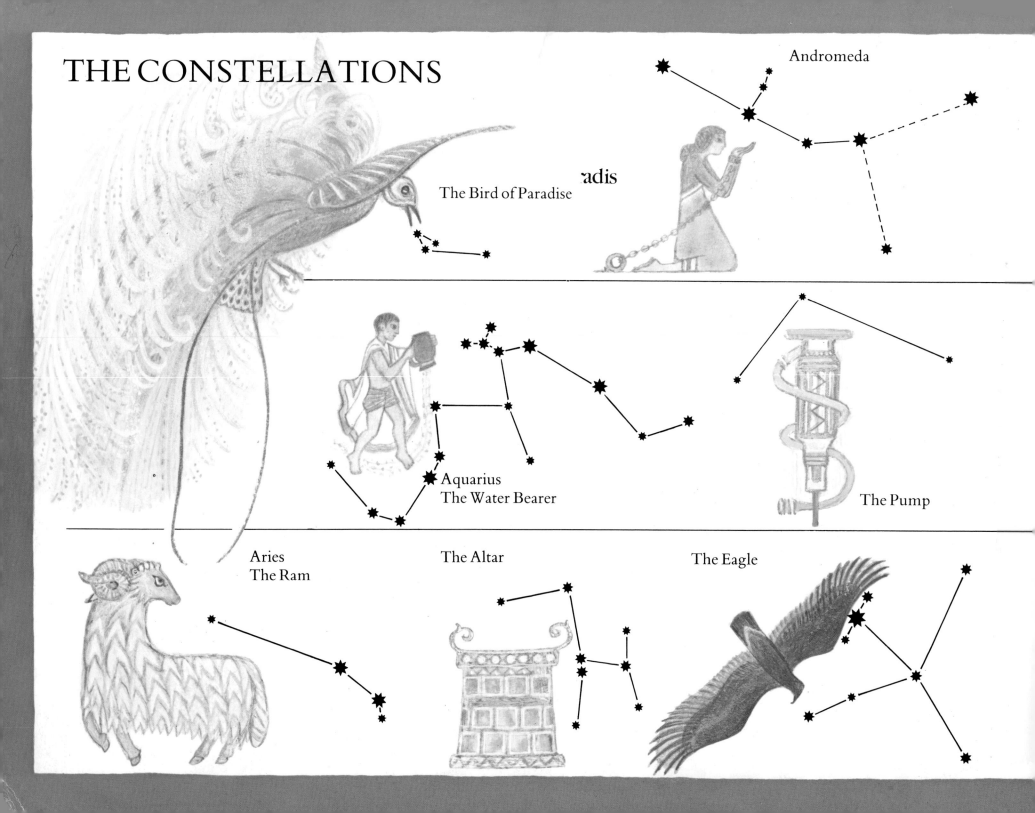

Andromeda

The Bird of Paradise

Aquarius
The Water Bearer

The Pump

Aries
The Ram

The Altar

The Eagle

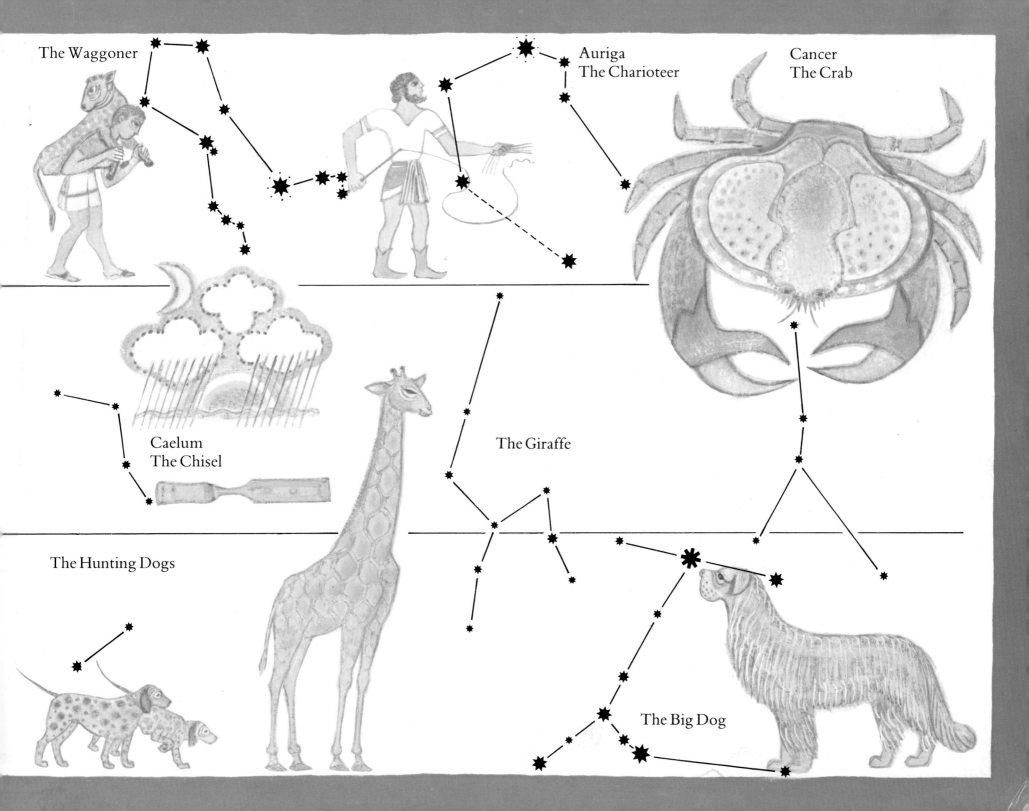

The Waggoner

Auriga
The Charioteer

Cancer
The Crab

Caelum
The Chisel

The Giraffe

The Hunting Dogs

The Big Dog

THE WINGED HORSE

Pegasus and Perseus

A lone seagull was flying over the barren country of Kisthene, swooping, soaring, a bright, white streak in the gathering dusk.

All at once there was a swift movement below. Medusa the Gorgon darted out of hiding, and her stony glance pierced the seagull like an arrow, and turned it to solid rock. The bird fell headlong out of the sky.

Medusa and her sister-Gorgons ran capering over the rocks, snarling and clawing as the fought over the dead bird. Stone prey: their joy and their delight since time began…

A thousand miles away, Perseus sat talking with three gods: Hades, Hermes and Athene. "Perseus," said Athene, "you must kill Medusa, and bring back her sliced-off head. Borrow Hermes' winged sandals, to carry you to her lair. Take Hades' helmet of invisibility to help you creep up on her unseen. And take my mirror-shield, to save you from her stony glance."

The gods vanished, and Perseus buckled on his sword, and put Hades' helmet on his head and Hermes' sandals on his feet. Then he took Athene's glittering shield and flew, wind-fast, to Kisthene and the Gorgons' lair.

The three Gorgons were snuffling and snorting in their cave, asleep. Their snake-hair bristled at the whirr of Perseus' winged sandals. But he was invisible: unaware of danger, Medusa and her sisters slept on.

Perseus turned his back on the Gorgons. Then he held up Athene's mirror-shield to guide his movements behind his back. He lifted his sword and sliced off Medusa's head. It fell on the floor, and the deadly eyes flicked open. If Perseus had been looking straight at them, he would have been turned to stone.

He stuffed the head into a sack. Then he jumped back in amazement. Out of the blood from Medusa's neck a winged horse, Pegasos, was appearing and growing before his eyes.

Pegasos stretched his wings, whinnied and pawed the ground. Then, to Perseus' surprise, he spoke human words. "Quick, Perseus! Jump on my back. Hurry!"

Perseus scrambled on to Pegasos' back, and Pegasos reared and beat his wings for take-off. The sound woke the sleeping Gorgons, and he soared away just in the nick of time, leaving them clawing angrily at empty air.

Pegasos carried Perseus safely home, and set him down in a grassy field. Then he soared away to his master Zeus, high in Olympos. Perseus watched him climbing higher and higher, like a dazzling constellation in the sky.

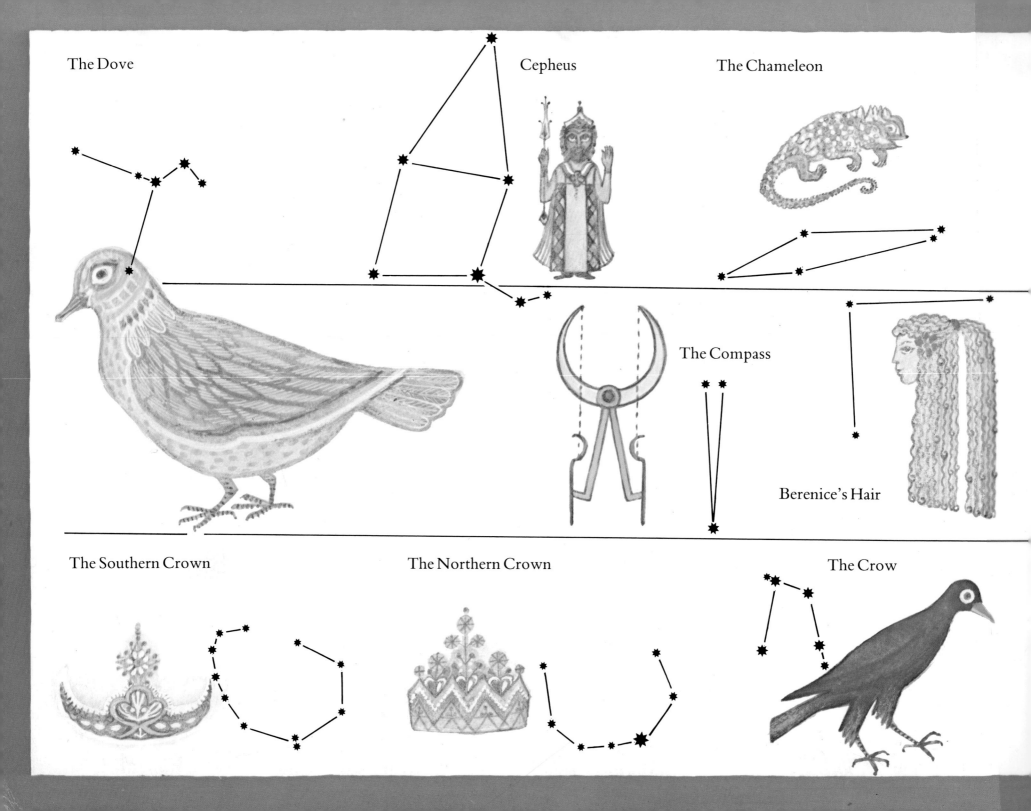

The Dove

Cepheus

The Chameleon

The Compass

Berenice's Hair

The Southern Crown

The Northern Crown

The Crow

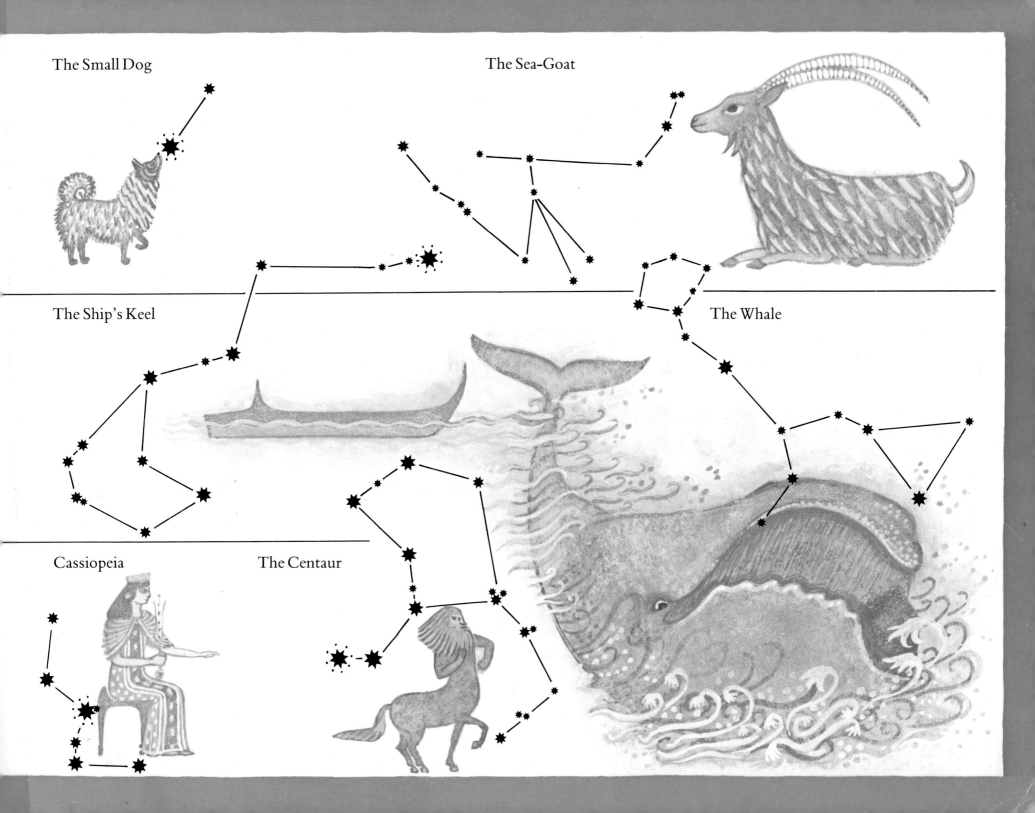

The Small Dog

The Sea-Goat

The Ship's Keel

The Whale

Cassiopeia

The Centaur

THE MIRACULOUS SHIP

The Ship's Keel

The Sails

The Ship's Stern

In an open space in front of his cave, the old centaur Cheiron was saying goodbye to one of his pupils. The young man was Jason, prince of Pherai in Greece. Long ago his wicked uncle Pelias had stolen Jason's throne and banished him. Now Jason was grown-up, and it was time to win back his throne.

For days Jason walked along rocky roads and across dusty, lonely plains. He was dressed in a panther-skin, and carried a spear in each hand. He wore a pair of new leather sandals – until one day, helping an old woman across a river, he lost one of them in the mud.

At last he came to Pherai. No one recognised him: he had been only a baby when he was banished, and now he was a handsome, grown-up prince. But Pelias guessed who he was. The gods had told him to beware of a young man wearing one sandal and an animal-skin tunic, and carrying a spear in each hand.

Instead of killing Jason outright, Pelias asked him a cunning question. "Stranger," he said, "if a stranger claimed your throne, what test would you set him to prove himself?"

"I'd send him to Colchis, to kill the dragon and fetch the Golden Fleece," answered Jason.

"You've chosen your own fate," said Pelias. "*You* claim my throne; *you* must sail to Colchis and fetch the fleece."

Jason knew that the voyage to Colchis would be long and dangerous. He would need fifty companions, the bravest heroes in Greece. And to carry them, he would need the finest ship ever built. He asked advice from Athene, goddess of wisdom.

"Find Argos," she said. "He's the best craftsman in Greece. He'll build you a ship strong enough to ride out every storm, swift enough to outsail the winds."

Argos set to work. He cut down fifty pine trees on Mount Pelion, trimmed them and shaped them into tough, curved planks. He pegged them together to make the ship. When it was nearly finished, Athene brought the last piece of timber and laid it in place. It was cut from Zeus' own sacred oak tree, and it had the magic power to speak and to foretell the future. As another sign of the gods' favour, Athene set a constellation of stars in the sky, and called it the Ship, in honour of Jason's mortal ship and the brave men who were to sail in it.

Jason called his ship *Argo,* after its maker Argos, and named its crew of heroes the Argonauts. When everything was ready, they launched *Argo,* took their places on the rowing-benches, and set off on their journey to find the Golden Fleece.

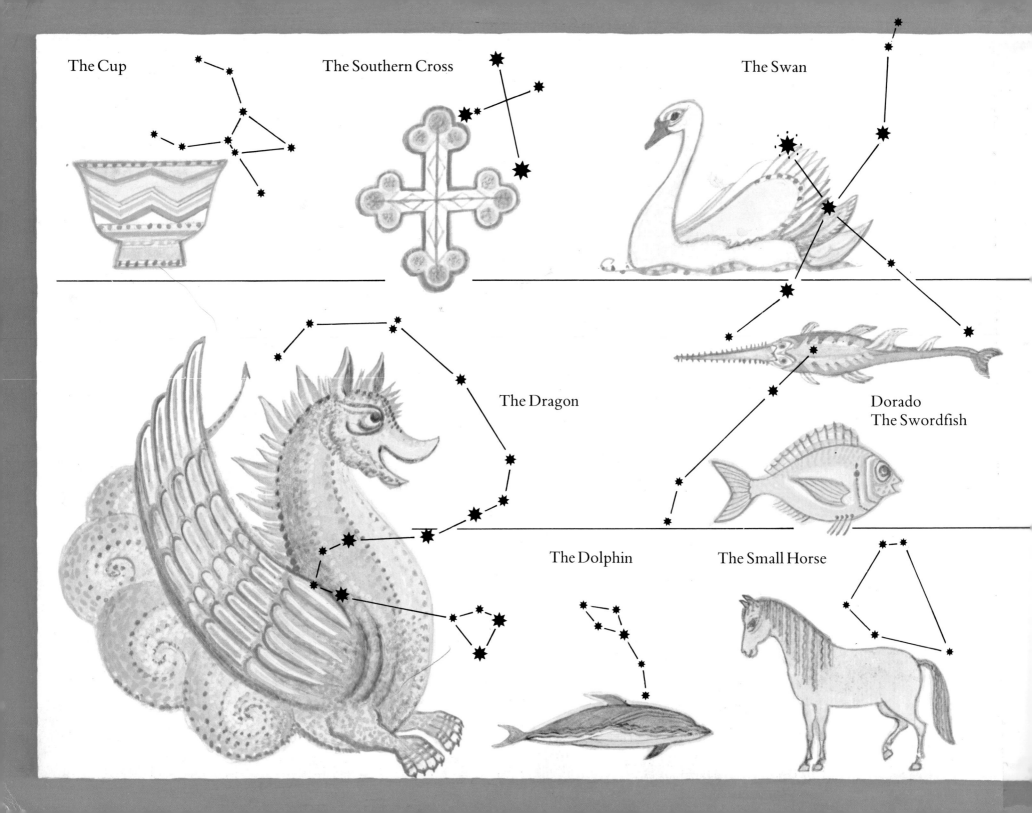

The Cup

The Southern Cross

The Swan

The Dragon

Dorado
The Swordfish

The Dolphin

The Small Horse

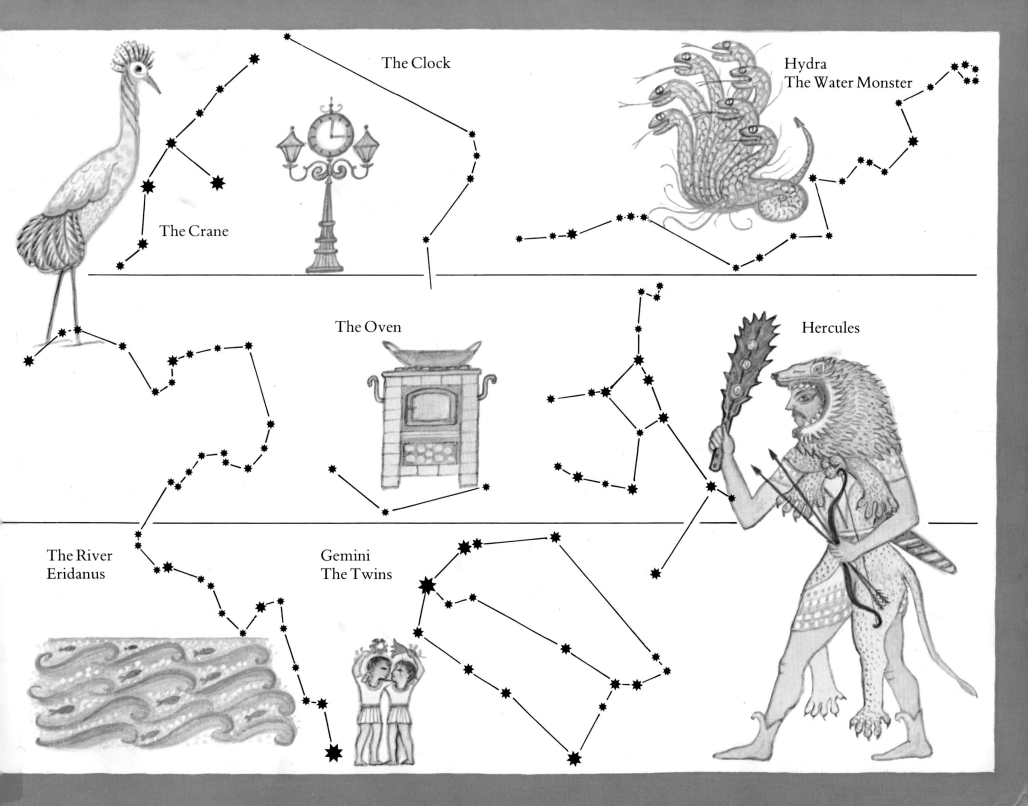

The Clock

Hydra
The Water Monster

The Crane

The Oven

Hercules

The River
Eridanus

Gemini
The Twins

THE YOUNGER BROTHER

Demeter, goddess of harvest, married a poor farmer called Iasion. Their land was dry and hard, and before Iasion could dig it he had to break up lumps of clay and move away twigs and branches scattered by the wind. He spent his days filling a hand-cart and pulling it to the rubbish-tip, back and forth, back and forth, from dawn to dusk.

Demeter and Iasion had two sons, Ploutos and Philomelos. Ploutos was blind, and Philomelos looked after him, guiding his steps and calling out to help him as they played in the fields and woods.

Although Ploutos was the eldest, there was no way a blind person could run a farm. Philomelos knew that one day, when he grew up, he would become the man of the house in his father's place. He wondered what his poor blind brother would find to do.

But Zeus had plans for Ploutos. One day, when the brothers were resting in the shade, Hermes the messenger-god flew down to them. He was carrying the magic Horn of Plenty. It was brimming with treasure, and could never be emptied: new riches always bubbled up to keep it full.

"Ploutos," said Hermes, "Zeus asks you to share this wealth out among all human beings. Take the Horn, and wherever you find people who deserve to be wealthy, give them a share of treasure. As you're blind, you'll find good people only by chance. No one will be able to say that the God of Wealth has eyes only for those he likes."

The Waggoner

Hermes gave Ploutos the Horn of Plenty, and a stick to guide his steps as he wandered through the world. Then he vanished. Sadly, Philomelos found his brother a cloak for his journey, a knapsack, sandals, and a wide-brimmed hat to keep off the sun. He guided him to the track which led out of the farm, and saw him safely on his way.

Though Philomelos loved his brother, he was jealous. Why should Zeus favour Ploutos, and not him? Ploutos was to help mortals by giving them wealth – what could *he* give them, stuck at home on his

father's farm? He climbed a tree to watch until Ploutos was out of sight. As he sat there, his cattle began to gather at the foot of the tree, waiting patiently for Philomelos to lead them home.

As Philomelos sat in the tree, wondering what gift he could possible find for mortals, he began absent-mindedly twisting and bending one of the branches. All at once it snapped, and fell on two astonished cows below.

Philomelos' eyes gleamed with a sudden idea. He jumped out of the tree, pulled down some creepers and another branch, and set to work.

Later, back at the farmhouse, Demeter was peeling vegetables, wondering why Iasion and the boys were so late home. Then she heard crows cawing outside, the rattle of wagon-wheels, and Philomelos' excited shouts. She gaped in surprise. Instead of plodding home exhausted, pulling his heavy hand-cart, Iasion walked whistling up the path, with his mattock slung over one shoulder. Beside him, Philomelos led a pair of oxen. They were yoked with creepers and branches, and harnessed to Iasion's wagon, which was piled high with wood.

Philomelos had found a gift for mortals just as useful as his brother's wealth. He had invented the yoke. Men no longer had to pull heavy loads by hand: they could harness cattle, and let them do the work. To show her joy at this invention, Demeter placed a constellation of stars, the Waggoner, to trundle forever across the sky.

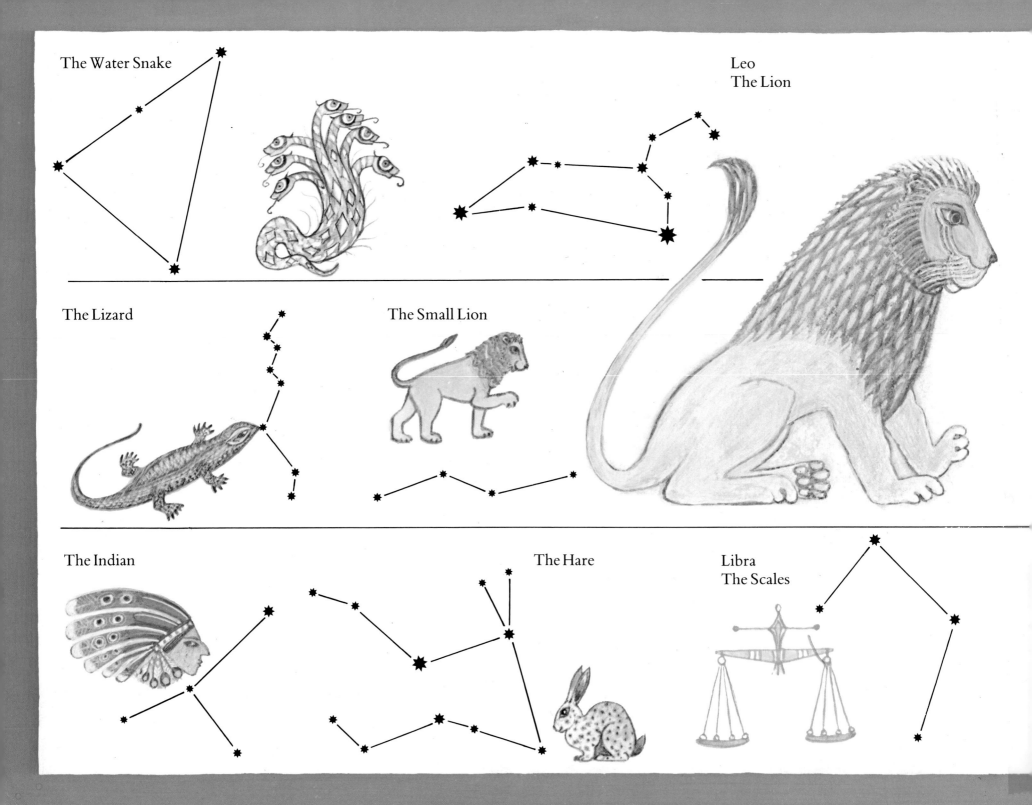

The Water Snake

Leo
The Lion

The Lizard

The Small Lion

The Indian

The Hare

Libra
The Scales

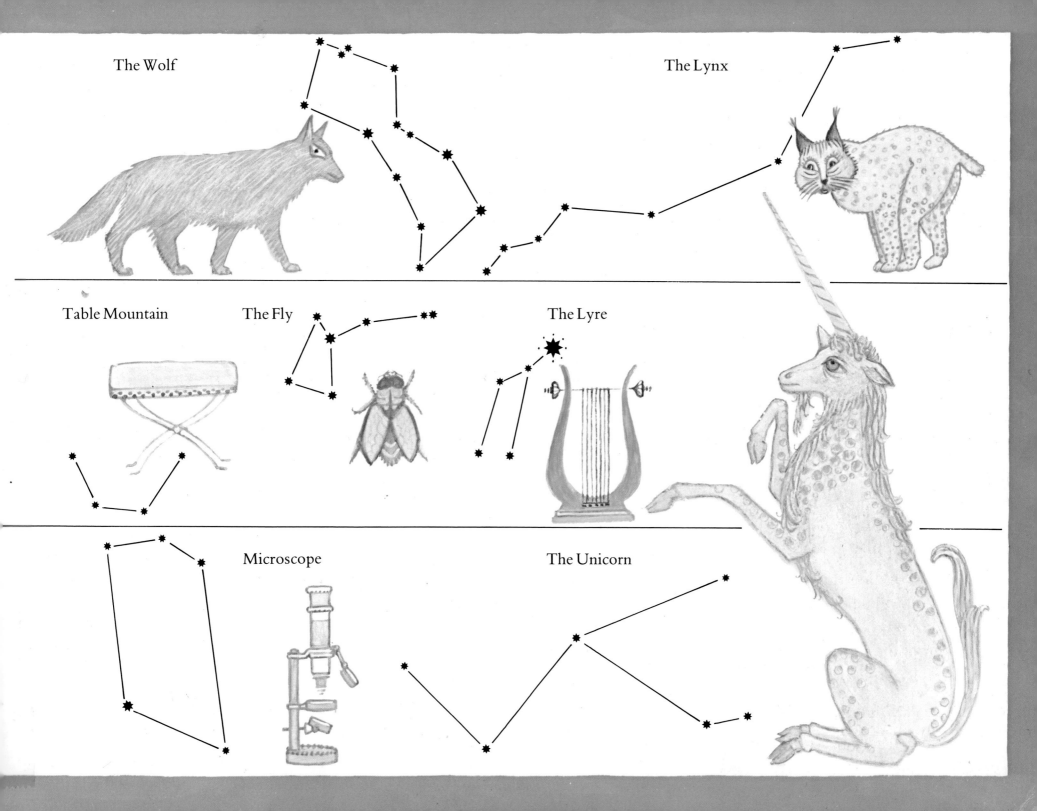

The Wolf

The Lynx

Table Mountain

The Fly

The Lyre

Microscope

The Unicorn

THE WEDDING-GIFT

The Northern Crown

From a seashell in a rock-pool by the shore, a tiny hermit-crab scuttled out of hiding. It began sidling busily up the beach. Then something blocked its path, and it gripped hold and began to climb over it.

The something was the foot of Ariadne, pricess of Crete. She was lying on the sand, fast asleep. When she felt the crab's tiny pincers, she jumped up with a scream, wide awake. Then, as she saw the deserted shore, and the silhouette of a ship disappearing out to sea, she burst into tears. Her sobs filled the air; there was no answer but the ripple of waves against the shore.

The day before, Ariadne had helped Theseus kill the Minotaur, deep in the tunnels of the Cretan labyrinth. The labyrinth was a maze,

a honeycomb of passages no one could pick his way through unhelped. Ariadne gave Theseus a ball of wool; he unravelled it as he went into the maze, and wound it up to guide his steps out again.

Theseus escaped with Ariadne to the lonely island of Naxos. He even promised to marry her. But then she fell asleep, and he sailed away and left her alone on the empty shore.

All day Ariadne wandered sadly among the rocks and sand-dunes. There was no one: no fisherman, no shepherd, no family picknicking on the beach. At last evening came, and in the gathering dark Ariadne began walking across a wide, bare plain. Perhaps there were houses, and people to welcome her, on the other side.

As she walked, the air suddenly filled with light and the laughter and singing of a procession. The god Dionysos galloped down the sky in a chariot pulled by two prancing panthers. His satyrs followed in a noisy dance.

Dionysos halted his chariot beside Ariadne. He took her hand, and spoke to her with kind words of love.

"Ariadne, come with me. I want you to be my queen, and live with me in Olympos. The gods are preparing our wedding-feast."

Back on the beach, the little hermit-crab was picking its way home to its rock-pool hiding-place. All at once its eyes, bulging on their stalks, were dazzled by a glittering light. A new constellation was gleaming in the sky: Dionysos' wedding-present to his beloved Ariadne, a jewel-and-diamond-encrusted crown.

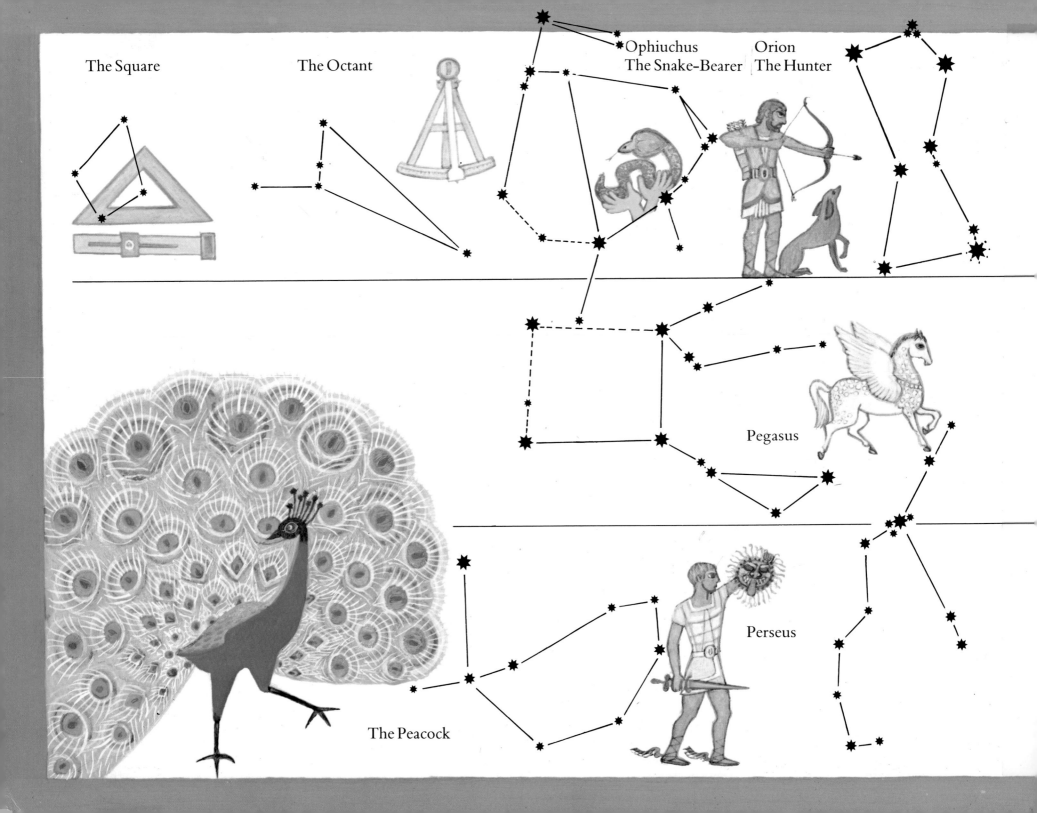

The Square

The Octant

Ophiuchus
The Snake-Bearer

Orion
The Hunter

Pegasus

The Peacock

Perseus

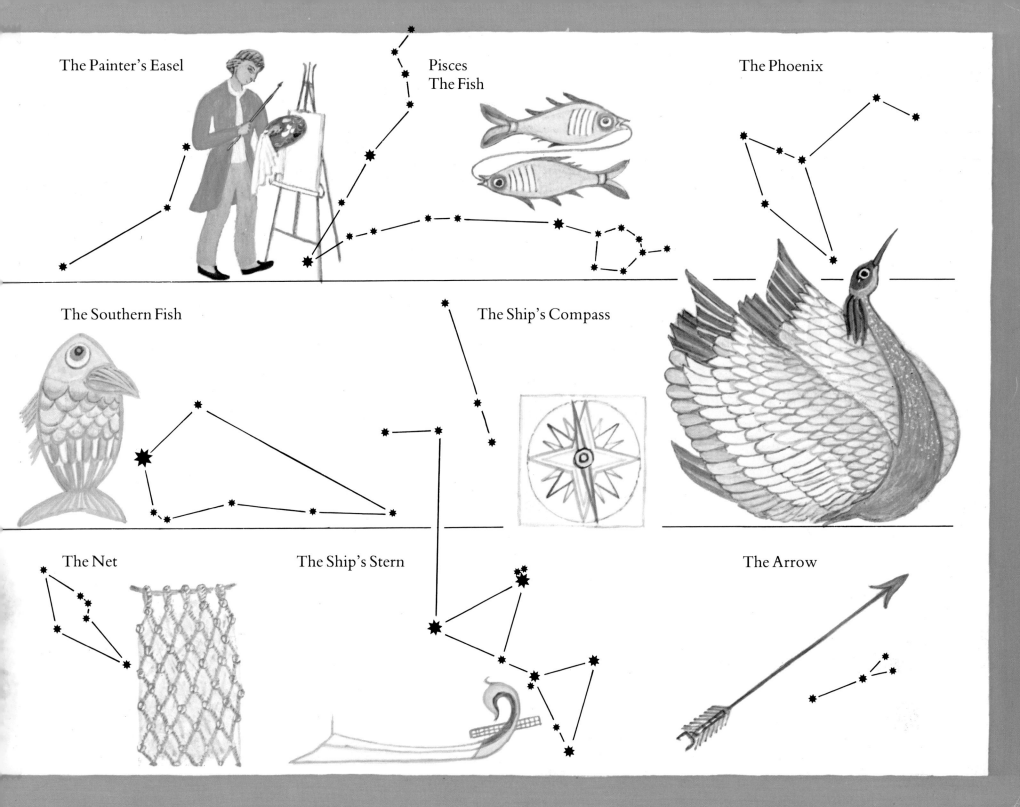

The Painter's Easel

Pisces
The Fish

The Phoenix

The Southern Fish

The Ship's Compass

The Net

The Ship's Stern

The Arrow

HERA'S ANGER

In a sunny summer field, Zeus and Hermes were hay-making. They had flown down from Olympos, disguised as mortals. They were helping the farmer by forking the loose hay up and fastening it into stooks.

At the edge of the field, baby Herakles was watching a bird tugging at an earthworm, trying to dislodge it from the ground. Herakles gurgled with delight. He grasped the worm in one chubby hand, hauled it out and handed it to the astonished bird.

"Look, Hermes," said Zeus. "Look how strong he is, even as a baby. He's Herakles, my mortal son. I wish I could make him immortal, and bring him to Olympos to live with the gods. But his mother is a mortal woman, and it's the mother's milk which makes a baby mortal or immortal."

"Leave it to me," said Hermes. He changed in an instant from being mortal into a god. His winged sandals carried him fluttering across to Herakles. He picked up the delighted baby in both arms, swung him on his back, and flew up with him to Olympos.

That night Hera, queen of the gods, slept restlessly. She dreamed that she and Zeus had a new baby, and that he was forever waking her up in the middle of the night, demanding to be fed. In her dream, she could even feel him at her breast, sucking her milk.

Hera woke up with a start. There *was* a baby at her breast, a real baby – Herakles. Hermes had crept in as Hera slept, and laid Herakles beside her to suck her milk.

Herakles! A mortal baby, sucking the milk that would make him immortal! Furiously Hera hurled him away from her. He fell into Hermes' waiting arms, and was carried gently back to earth, floating down as lightly as a feather.

Hera went crossly back to bed. And drops of milk, shaken from her breast, spilled out across the evening sky. At once they turned into stars and constellations: the ones ever afterwards called The Milky Way.

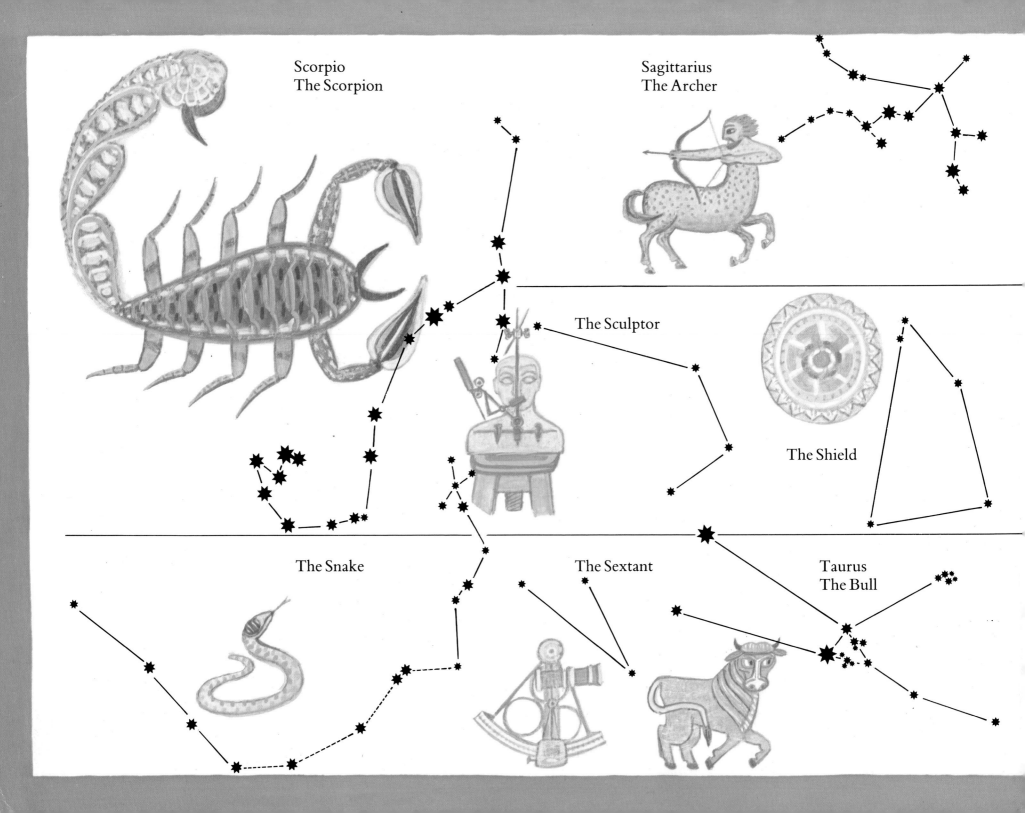

Scorpio
The Scorpion

Sagittarius
The Archer

The Sculptor

The Shield

The Snake

The Sextant

Taurus
The Bull

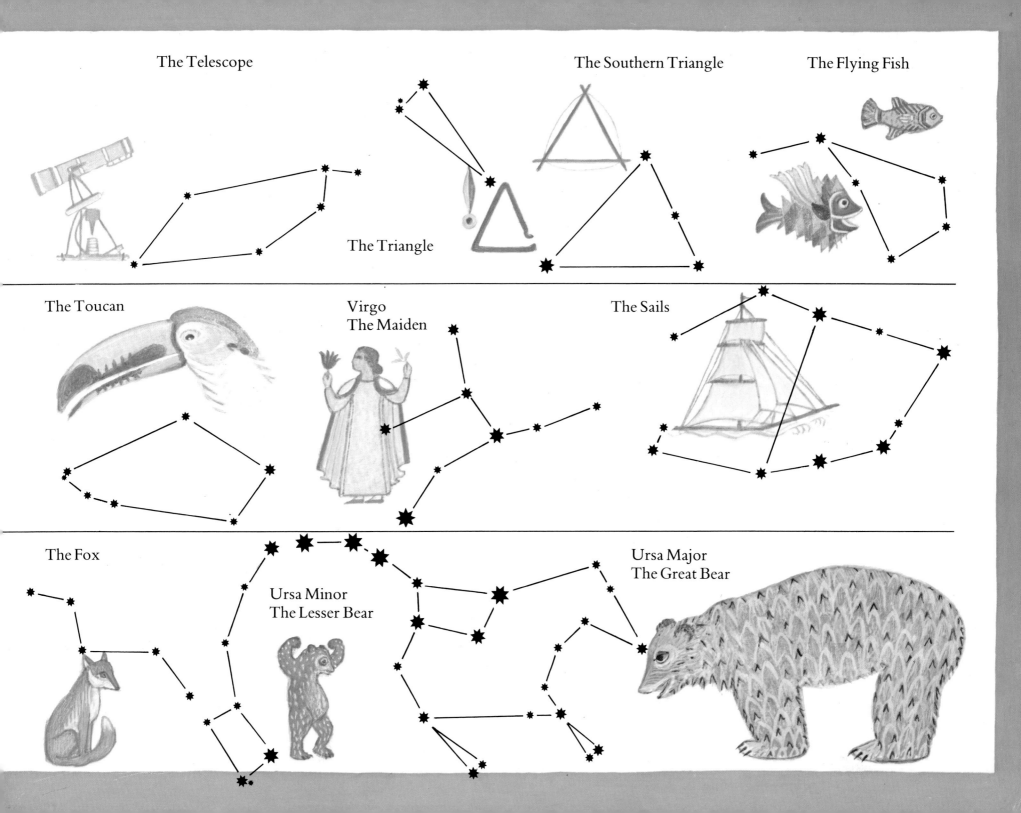

The Telescope

The Southern Triangle

The Flying Fish

The Triangle

The Toucan

Virgo
The Maiden

The Sails

The Fox

Ursa Minor
The Lesser Bear

Ursa Major
The Great Bear

HOW TO MAKE YOUR OWN STAR-SHOW

In a planetarium, a projector shows light-pictures of the heavenly bodies on a dome-shaped ceiling. It shows planets, stars, and constellations – as they used to be, their positions now, and their possible future movements. The pictures are made up of blobs and patterns of light, some bright, some faint. They imitate the shape and size of real heavenly bodies, seen with the naked eye.

A proper planetarium is complicated and expensive to install. But you can make a simple star-show to use in your own home.

All you need is a bicycle lamp or pocket torch, four pins, a cardboard tube and some pieces of paper with holes pricked in them. Switch off the lights, lie back in bed, and make star-patterns on the walls and ceiling of your own bedroom.

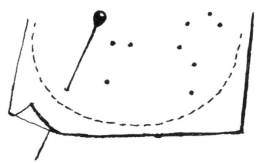

1. On a piece of paper, draw the star-pattern of one of the constellations (e.g. Leo, the Lion).

2. At the place where each star comes in the pattern, prick a hole in the paper with a pin. (Make the holes the right size: some stars are bigger than others and will need a bigger hole.)

3. Pin the star-map to the end of the cardboard tube.

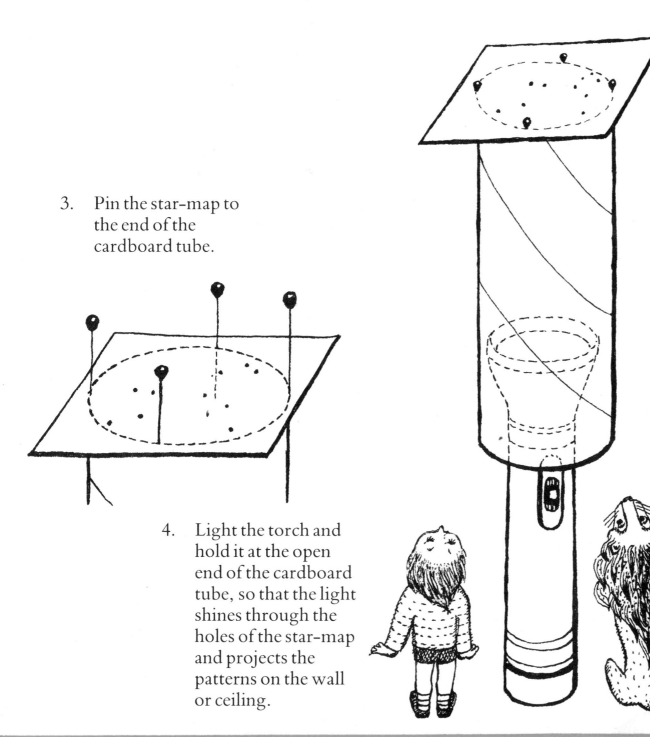

4. Light the torch and hold it at the open end of the cardboard tube, so that the light shines through the holes of the star-map and projects the patterns on the wall or ceiling.

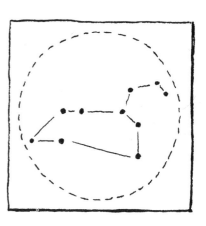

5. You can project a new constellation by changing the paper star-map.
The narrower your cardboard tube, the brighter the picture it will project.

STAR-MAPS OF THE WORLD

If you live in the northern hemisphere, during the year you can see the whole of the northern sky (that is, all the stars and constellations north of the equator), and all of the southern sky as far as ninety degrees south of your parallel. ("Parallels" are lines drawn across star-maps, parallel to the equator. So if you live in Cairo, you are on the 30° parallel north and during the year you can see all the northern stars and the southern stars as far as the 60° parallel south.)

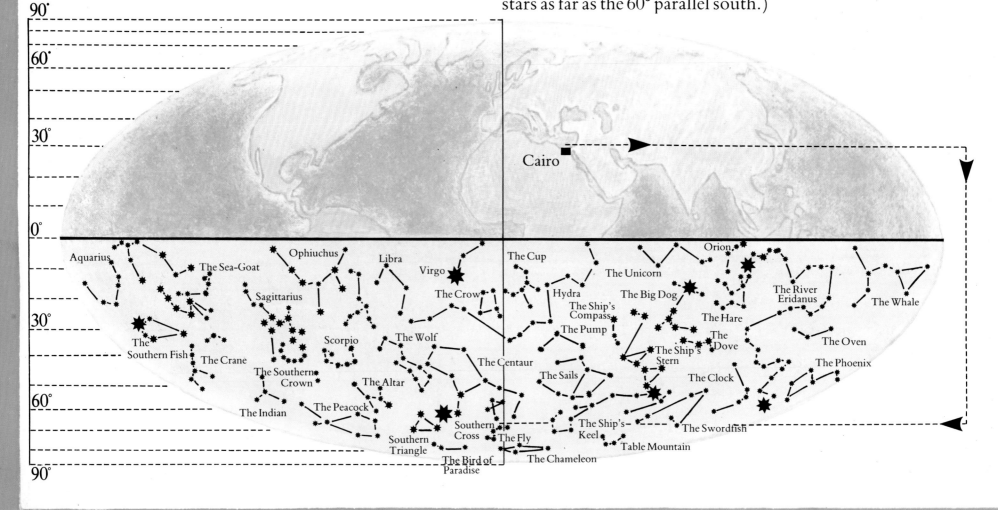

If you live in the southern hemisphere, during the year you can see the whole of the southern sky and all the northern sky as far as ninety degrees north of your parallel. (So, if you live in the Cape, you are on the 35° parallel south, and can see all the southern stars plus all the northern stars as far as the 55° parallel north.)

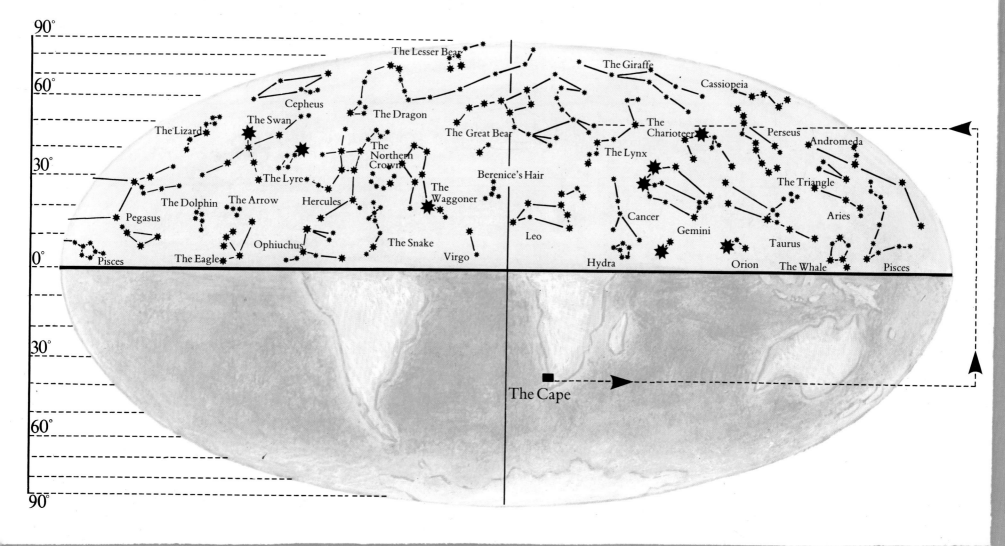

ABOUT THE STARS

The stars in the night sky are really distant suns. Each twinkling speck is a giant ball of glowing gas, like our own sun, but very much further away. Every day, the planet we live on, Earth, turns round once. Day comes to the places on the side of Earth facing the sun. On the other side of the Earth there is darkness and night. As the Earth spins, the sun rises in the eastern sky every morning. It sets again in the west as evening comes.

The stars, too, rise and set. The constellations that can be seen in the east after sunset gradually climb and cross the sky during the course of the night. All the time, new stars are rising over the horizon. It is easy to check the moving stars on a clear night.

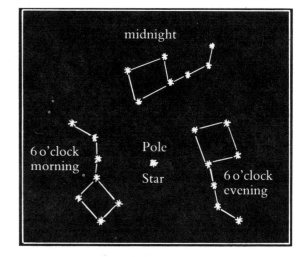

Position of the Great Bear at different times at the end of March.

Each star rises four minutes earlier every day. This means that the constellations which can be seen in the evening change with the seasons of the year. But there are some stars that can always be seen. Those near the north or south pole of the sky never set. The Great Bear in the north and the Cross in the south are constellations that are always up. If you watched all night, you would see them swing half way round the sky.

The movement of the star patterns across the sky over an hour or two.